FREE and Open Source Software,

an Enabler for Strategic Alignment through Tactical and Operational Factors

B. Charles Henry

Information Technology Manager & Adjunct Lecturer

Contents

Preface   v

Author's Biography   ix

Chapter 1

Leadership Roles   1

Alignment Factors of Leadership Roles   2

IS Roles in Organizations – An Example   3

Achieving Strategic Advantage through Tactical and Operational Roles   5

Strategic Innovation Examples   7

Lessons Learned   12

Conclusion   14

References   16

Chapter 2

FOSS, an Enabler for Strategic Alignment Through Tactical/Operational Factors   18

Historical Development   21

Contemporary Best Practices   26

Emerging Trends and Opportunities   32

Conclusion   38

References   42

Chapter 3

Collaboration   50

Learning Teams   51

Changes   52

Give Suggestions Freely   53

Improving Collaboration   54

Conclusion   55

References   57

Chapter 4

Questions and Answers   59

Why Invest in New Technology   59

Advantages/Disadvantages of Pioneering Technology   61

References   62

What are the Conditions for Open Source Viability   63

References   66

What Constitute the Free Economy   68

    References   71

How Does Collaborative Learning and Content
    Management Benefit IT   72

    References   74

What is Innovation of Information Systems   75

    Conclusion   76

    References   78

What are Fitness Landscapes   79

    References   82

What is the Importance of Good Network Design   83

    Conclusion   85

    References   86

What are the Ethics of Wireless Network Discovery   87

    References   90

What are 4G Broadband   92

    References   95

Are There Opportunities for Blogging   97

    References   100

What are the Benefits of SaaS & Cloud Computing   101

    SaaS   102

    References   103

What is Business Intelligence & Intellectual Property   104

    Intellectual Property   105

    References   107

What is Simulation-based Acquisition   109

    References   110

What is Crowd Sourcing & Cognitive Surplus   111

    Cognitive Surplus   112

    References   114

How Does Disruptive Technology Influence
    Software Development   116

    References   119

What is the Danger with Ambiguity and
    Systems Development   120

References   123

Reader's Notes Page   124

Preface

Free and open source software (FOSS) provides an immense opportunity to leverage the cost of information systems and technology implementation, maintenance, and management. Considering the prevailing circumstances as it relates to investments in information systems infrastructure, it becomes prudent, now more than ever, to assess the appropriateness of information systems costs and by extension, the returns of such investments. The cost of information systems and technology is ballooning out of control as the useful life of technology implementation becomes shorter as we advance into the new decades. Information systems and technology (IST) managers therefore have an obligation to seek out alternative source of technology innovation to keep their businesses operating at an optimal level.

With these concerns in mind, I present a short report addressing issues such as the organizational roles and alignment factors to consider in driving information technology investments. In addition, I have organized an outstanding bibliography of researchers and field experts in the domain that can further assist in the smooth transition from an overly costly proprietary genre to free and open source software. I have included a series of questions and answers that may be of assistance to the reader is helping him or her to galvanize the support and benefit of FOSS. Because the intention of the book is to provide guidance to the reader, I have followed each section immediately with its references for further probity and assessment of the argument presented without having to flip back and forth between the respective chapters and the back of the book. No additional reference pages are included.

Each section of the book stands alone. It is not therefore the intention of the author for the reader to read the book from cover to cover, though it is a light read and would not hinder understanding. The author's intention is to offer some practical guide to FOSS implementation rather than to present a theoretical construct that reads like a novel from cover to cover. Enough of those exist. The objective here is to engage the reader to participate in the discourse and to make the transition from an academic discussion to implementation and management of a technology that has proven its readiness, sustainability, and maturity for the information and communications technology sector.

The book is only a few pages of easy read and one hopes that there will be some enjoyment in sifting through the materials presented and that a lively discussion will ensue. I bid all readers a productive and engaging reading exercise. The book is also ideal for undergraduates and postgraduates pursuing a foundation information systems course, an introductory management or leadership courses.

Author's Biography

The author originates from Jamaica in the West Indies. He holds a Bachelor of Science degree with majors in Accounting and Management Studies and a Master's of Science degree in Computer Based Management Information Systems, both from the University of the West Indies, Mona campus in Kingston, Jamaica. The author is currently pursuing doctoral studies in Organizational Leadership with specialization in Information Systems and Technology.

The author is an Information Technology Manager and an Adjunct Lecturer in various information systems courses. The author achieved the Who's Who of Professionals recognition in 2001. In 2002, he was nominated a Mover and Shaker in the premier local daily newspaper. He is a full member of IEEE Computer Society

and a member of the Jamaica Computer Society.

Leadership Roles

In order for an organization to carry out its many functions, organizations vest in various persons certain responsibilities. These responsibilities or *roles* are behavior types intended to achieve organizational objectives. Typically, four types of roles exist within organizations. These roles include task roles intended to achieve the group's objectives; maintenance roles that focus on the group's socio-economic climate; individual roles that pays attention to self ("Group/organization roles", n.d.) and leadership roles that "facilitate activities of and relationships in a group or organization" (Yukl, p. 3). This essay will focus on the responsibilities that leadership undertakes in organizations.

Alignment Factors of Leadership Roles

As organizations rely more heavily on information technology (IT), the need for the technology's strategic alignment with organizational objectives becomes more crucial. Organizations are more discerning of information technology investments that will enhance competitiveness and improve organizational performance (Gutierrez, Orozco, Serrano, & Serrano, 2006). Three major alignment roles or competitive advantages are available to assist a leader achieve his or her objectives. First, strategic advantage (alignment) endeavor to establish a nexus between business and IT visions. The organization applies technology that will improve business performance and competitiveness (Gutierrez et al., 2006). Second, an organization achieves tactical advantage (alignment) when its strategies perform better than its competitors do

(McLeod & Schell, 2007). Third, organizations achieve operational advantage (alignment) when they improve their business rules for effective daily operations (McLeod & Schell, 2007).

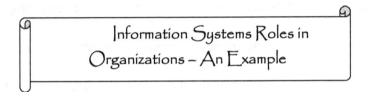

Information Systems Roles in
Organizations – An Example

Let us use an example from a hypothetical law firm to help the illustration. The firm uses technology primarily for two objectives, tactical, and operational goals. The firm strives to achieve tactical advantage by using advanced technology for case management and conflict management. For case management, the firm can quickly, through a few clicks of the mouse, state exactly where a case is in the system, to what department the case belong, and the lawyer handling the matter. Depending on how the matter is progressing, the executives may quickly assess if the advancement of the case is reasonable or whether they should transfer the matter to another lawyer. In conflict management, the firm cannot accept a new case from someone or an organization if the firm already represents another person or organization, subsidiary, or any other connected parties. Lawyers accepting the case may quickly query the database of all matters to ascertain if such connection may exist. Because of this feature in the software, the lawyer can return a prompt response to the person or organization so enquiring, whether it is possible to accept his or her case.

For operational advantage, the firm strives to make daily use and management of the technology at users console as simple and user-friendly as possible. The firm strives to deliver unparallel service and turnaround time to clients because the firm wants clients to "come back to us" each time the clients meet challenges requiring the services of a lawyer. The firm's law-practice management software helps to achieve such an objective. The software's functional richness delivers the requirements of the most sophisticated practices with efficiency and ease of use. The software delivers unparalleled performance to the users' desktop.

Technology and business operations must be aligned to achieve innovative and strategic competitiveness. Therefore, the information technology manager must assist the firm to reach its strategic goals through the application and use of both tactical and operational roles as highlighted above.

Achieving Strategic Advantage through Tactical and Operational Roles

The use of tactical and operational roles to leverage strategic advantage encompasses two perspectives. First, an alignment that supports relevance to business performance and IT benefits to business operations. Second, how the alignment helps the existing circumstances to improve. From the law-practice management software example outlined above, it should be clear that the firm's approach is the use of tactical and operational means to leverage strategic advantages for the organization.

The firm recognizes the interconnectedness and interdependence of both technology and business. The firm operates under the premise that technology and business co-constitute each other. The reciprocity of both creates the possibilities for strategic outcome (Stanford University, 2005). In the context of how the firm operates, the IT Manager is not at liberty to do whatever he or she may, but should act within the purview of the strategic direction of the firm.

Strategic Innovation Examples

Nortel Networks implemented knowledge management technology to transform its business operations from a technology-focused organization to a customer-focused organization (McLeod & Schell, 2007). Knowledge management engages the activities of "acquiring data, processing data into information, using and communicating information in the most effective way, and discarding information at the proper time" (McLeod & Schell, 2007, p. 34). Nortel achieved this transformation by creating a new product (NPD) that "(1) leverage multidisciplinary NPD knowledge assets, (2) improve NPD decision making, and (3) facilitate learning and knowledge exchange" (McLeod & Schell, 2007, p. 87).

United Parcel Service (UPS) a distribution and courier service company promised its customers the "best service and lowest rates" (Laudon & Laudon, 2007, p. 20). UPS achieved this promise by using a strategic alignment of technology and business operations. UPS coupled its automated package tracking system with a handheld computer called a "Delivery Information Acquisition Device (DIAD)" (Laudon & Laudon, 2007, p. 20). The DIAD allow the UPS drivers to upload automatically the delivery information to its central processing locations for immediate processing. Customers that query the status of their delivery have instantaneous notification.

FedEx a distribution and courier service company "created a first-mover advantage by creating its customer self-service software" (Baltzan & Phillips, 2009, p. 17). This first-mover tracking software allowed FedEx customers to requests pickups, track packages, and print their own mailing labels, all accommodated through an online portal (Baltzan & Phillips, 2009). The move by FedEx at the time was radical and disruptive. Customers saw the need and quickly began to use the services which launched FedEx as a major distribution and courier service company.

Accenture, a global consulting and outsourcing services firm, has no physical headquarters or branches. Every negotiations and customer service management goes through the company's web portal, e-mails, and telephones (Laudon & Laudon, 2007). By combining virtualization with outsourcing, Accenture avoids overhead costs typically associated with maintaining huge buildings (Laudon & Laudon, 2007).

Kia Motors implemented a quality control system for its manufacturing process that "helps identify sources of defects in Kia automobiles" (Laudon & Laudon, 2007, p. 47). Kia then uses such information to correct the defects that led to better vehicles and improved customer satisfaction (Laudon & Laudon, 2007). Kia Motors, through the implementation of their quality control information systems, combined tactical and operational advantages to achieve strategic benefits in the marketplace.

Amazon.com is the "world's biggest bookstore" (Baltzan & Phillips, 2009, p. 64). Amazon operates no physical bookstore. It ships directly from its publishers and other traditional bookstores. Amazon's sales occur through its web portal. Amazon's use of technology for this e-business strategy allows Amazon to offer a wide range of titles that no traditional bookstore could offer. The number of titles creates an instant success for Amazon (Baltzan & Phillips, 2009).

Stikeman Elliott, an international law firm based in Canada, introduced technology to capture the knowledge of its lawyers so that the organization can share such knowledge between the various departments and its specialized areas when conducting business (Laudon & Laudon, 2007). Stikeman Elliott and Nortel believe that properly managed knowledge can create competitive advantage for the organization. Precedent knowledge is most crucial to lawyers. These precedents may come in the form of "documents, forms, guidelines, and best practices" (Laudon & Laudon, 2007, p. 442). Stikeman Elliott needed to capture such precedents for its effective and competitive operation.

Other companies using IT in these remarkable ways include Constellation Energy that use technology to "Connect. Interact. Transform" (Haag & Cummings, 2008, p. 77). 7-Eleven use technology to implement a state of art backup and recovery system (Baltzan & Phillips, 2009). The Canadian government uses technology for knowledge management. The government uses social networking analysis (SNA) "to establish which skills it needed to retain and develop, and to determine who ... had the most important knowledge and experience to begin transferring to others" (Baltzan & Phillips, 2009, p. 319). British Columbia Milk Marketing Board use technology to implement a decision support system that captures data in real time. This new technology enables reliable decision-making, and cost savings on paper and the antiquated accounting system previously used (Haag & Cummings, 2008).

Lessons Learned

From the various examples listed above, technology and business objectives drives the convergence and alignment roles of strategy, tactics, and operation. Visionary leaders possess skill-sets capable of changing their organization culture. Leadership is a process that "facilitate activities and relationships in a group or organization" (Yukl, p. 3). However, the kind of leadership demonstrated above through the respective examples, goes beyond a management style of leadership. Such leadership qualities incorporate vision and are thus transformational in their behavior and outlook. The chief executive officer (CEO) Jack Welch of General Electric during the 1980s posited that the new dispensation for businesses require "entrepreneurial, lean, and agile" abilities (Tichy & Devanna, 1990, p. 18). Welch further stated that "changing the culture – opening it up to quantum change – means constantly asking, not how fast I am going, how well am I doing versus how well I did a year or two years before, but rather how fast and how well am I doing versus the outside world?" (Tichy & Devanna, 1990, p. 18).

Conclusion

Technology and business must work together to provide opportunities that solve business problems. Whatever the alignment objective of businesses: strategic, tactical, or operational, the likelihood of businesses achieving these roles is inherent in leaders understanding the interconnectedness and interdependence of business and information systems and technology. Leaders should understand that business and technology forge a bond that accommodates the strategic objectives of organizations.

Contemporary leaders need to understand that the nature of today's businesses require a bit more than incremental change: that businesses should challenge the existing organizational culture to bring about radical and sustainable change that create new opportunities for both businesses and their customers alike. As demonstrated through the FedEx experience and the many examples above, businesses can and do create opportunities that customers do not recognize that they need until the option is presented to them.

As soon as organizations begin to engage visionary leaders, organizations will start reaping the benefit of such leadership in the way their businesses offer new opportunities and wealth creation for all the stakeholders alike, both owners, and customers. Until leaders understand their rightful place in the decision making process in organizations, the world will continue to see the exceptions, as those outlined above, rather than the visionary skills and activities that can truly shape daily business operations.

References

Baltzan, P., & Phillips, A. (2009). *Essentials of business driven information systems*. New York, NY: McGraw-Hill Irwin.

Group/organization roles. (n.d.). Retrieved July 8, 2010, from http://www.omniclass.org/tables/OmniClass_34_20 06-03-28.pdf

Gutierrez, A., Orozco, J., Serrano, A., & Serrano, A. (2006). *Using tactical and operational factors to assess strategic alignment: An SME study*. Retrieved July 8, 2010, from http://citeseerx.ist.psu.edu/

Haag, S., & Cummings, M. (2008). *Management information systems for the information age*. New York, NY: McGraw-Hill Irwin.

Laudon, K. C., & Laudon, J. P. (2007). *Management information systems* (10 ed.). Upper Saddle River, NJ: Pearson Prentice Hall.

McLeod, R., & Schell, G. (2007). *Management information systems* (10 ed.). Upper Saddle River, NJ: Pearson Prentice Hall.

Stanford University. (2005). *Phenomenological approaches to ethics and information technology.* Retrieved July 9, 2010, from http://plato.stanford.edu/entries/ethics-it-phenomenology/

Tichy, N. M., & Devanna, M. A. (1990). *The transformational leader: The key to global competitiveness.* New York, NY: John Wiley & Sons, Inc.

Yukl, G. (2006). *Leadership in organizations* (6th ed.). Upper Saddle River, NJ: Pearson Prentice Hall.

Free and Open Source Software, an Enabler for Strategic Alignment through Tactical/Operational Factors

Information systems and technology (IST) has the potential to advance business processes in mild or radical ways (Baltzan & Phillips, 2009). Whether businesses choose to accrue investment dollars in sustaining or radical endeavors, measurable benefits should justify every investment dollar. Hoving (2007) opined, "We genuinely recognize the value information technology can make if invested properly, but also acknowledge the problematic track record for successful projects" (Hoving, 2007, p. 150). Equally important is that information technology (IT) has long evolved beyond support functions. Today, technology serves enterprises as "both factory for their existing systems and turnaround for their systems development portfolio" (Hoving, 2007, p. 150).

Justifying IT investment costs however, is not necessarily an easy venture. Although there should be a clear relationship between processes and output, the realities prove otherwise. Other factors often blur the process of cost justification such as government regulations, firm structure, and firm size and may incorporate other complementary factors (Pavlou, Housel, Rodgers, & Jansen, 2005).

Because IT and related technology play such significant strategic role on daily business operations in contemporary economies, it behooves investment managers to ascertain that every investment dollar create wealth, enhance productivity, and engender competitiveness for the enterprise (Gutierrez, Orozco, Serrano, & Serrano, 2006). IST gives an enterprise a unique opportunity to incorporate the three major alignment roles or competitive advantages for business sustainability. First, managers should establish a clear nexus between business and IT visions (strategic) (Gutierrez et al., 2006). Second, managers want strategies that outperform their competitors (tactical). Third, managers want effective business rules for daily operations (operational) (McLeod & Schell, 2007). It would also seem reasonable to deduce that investment managers should demand the greatest "bang for their bucks."

Free and open source software (F/OSS) presents enterprises with many opportunities. Currently, many robust business applications are available under the GNU general public license (GPL.) For example, OpenOffice.org caters to governments, education, businesses, not for profits, IT businesses, and F/OSS advocates (OpenOffice.org, n.d.). Much software distributed under GPL license is "free" to acquire. In addition, open source software tends to enjoy a high quality because of the bazaar implementation methods such software has to endure (Raymond, 2000). Amazon.com, for example, "shelved millions of dollars from its technology costs last quarter [July-September, 2001] by switching to the Linux operating system" (Shankland, Kane, & Lemos, 2001, p. 1).

The following literature review is an attempt to support the hypothesis; F/OSS can use tactical and operational factors to enable organizations strategic alignment.

Historical Development

In a research article by Carillo and Okoli (2008), the authors articulated how skill-sets within the community of practice produce usable open source software to benefit both the community and the public at large. The authors spoke about the intellectual property rights benefits derived from "copyleft" because developers can publish their work under the GNU GPL. Copyleft "is the concept of making a program free software and requiring that all modified and extended versions of the program ... be free software as well" (Stinebrunner, Humphrey, & Davis, 2002, p. 18). The authors also provided evidence from the Journal of Computer Information Systems and articulated granular details for the community, organizations, and individuals.

Von Krogh (2003) assessed the innovative process and innovators incentives for developing F/OSS. Von Krogh (2003) gave a brief history of F/OSS and the GNU GPL. The author probed the reasons F/OSS attracts developers that would eagerly give away their intellectual property. The author discovered that the instant gratification developers achieve from peers act as a motivating factor for such developers to continue to give to the open source community. The author noted that because peer-review tends to improve the quality of the product, the process guarantees a high standard of quality and therefore, a more robust, and durable finished product.

Henkel (2009) argued that managers and developers spend unnecessary time arguing over intellectual property rights instead of seeing the true benefit of open source software. He concluded that whenever managers begin to take a positive assessment of open source software development and their potential benefit to the enterprises, better resource sharing would accrue to such organizations. The author provided numerous studies to support his argument.

O'Mahony (2007) examined the transition of open source at its inception to its current evolution transforming from a grassroots movement to an established community of practice incorporating major organizations. The author noted that private contributions to the open source software (OSS) community increased and hybrid systems are emerging. The author makes a distinction between OSS and the emerging hybrid systems. He emphasized the established governance of the open source community of practice.

Feinberg (2007) assessed the implications of collaborations among top technology firms and what effect such collaboration may have on open source database such as MySQL. Feinberg (2007) noted that such high-level collaboration propel the demand for open source databases. Feinberg (2007) opined that because of collaboration between IBM and MySQL, amongst others, many organizations joined the MySQL database initiative. The author however pointed out that a demand for technical expertise is somewhat limiting the rapid growth and deployment of open source databases.

Mears (2005) research focused on the growth of open source databases. The author noted that as companies seek new ways to address production costs they are more likely to pursue open source software development. She noted that the increased momentum to open source alternatives is an indication to the relative maturity of the open source market. Mears (2005) opined that established enterprises such as Dell, HP, and Novell offer MySQL options to their customers. Mears (2005) noted that because of the established standards within the open source community, enterprises could easily adapt services to their existing database infrastructure.

Contemporary Best Practices

Nomani, Cilimdzic, Fadden, and Chan (2009) research focused on a file system that provides flexibility and growth at a minimum cost. The authors also emphasized how developers can align such file system with best practices within the open source domain. The report incorporates how a program such as DB2 written specifically for the Linux open source platform can bring about scalability and manageability for technology professionals and enterprises. The authors enumerate specific benefits to include enhanced availability, dynamic infrastructure flexibility, continued high performance, and improved operational efficiency.

Reese (2002) researched and highlighted 10 best practices that technicians should consider when implementing MySQL databases. The author's major objectives include the importance of security to good database design, the critical role of maintenance, and other performance issues when working with an open source database such as MySQL. The author outlined very specific tasks that technicians should undertake throughout the implementation stage of the databases.

Barnett (2004) research focused on the increasing use of open source software to drive innovation with new products. Barnett (2004) opined reasons she believe open source development is working so effectively. The author noted that there exist no fundamental difference between the respective approaches to established agile methods and open source software (OSS) development life cycle. She further stated that management may need to assess such agile development methods to understand better why such methods are successful. The author stated however, that the process is not without challenge.

Barnett (2004) noted that some requirements might be difficult to achieve.

Hammond (2009) spoke about the renewed interests in open source development as organizations endeavor to cut development and operational budgets. Hammond (2009) noted that many software production facilities are already applying aspects of open source development, sometimes to the ignorance of the facilities managers. Hammond (2009) posited that organizations need policies and procedures to develop OSS. The author opined that wherever such policies exists, development professionals could then shift from a mode of tactical response to one of integration based on realistic demands and on the associated cost benefits.

Scacchi's (2003) presentation assessed best practices applicable to free and open source development (F/OSSD.) The author noted that F/OSSD should entail specific requirements and design specifications, configuration management, maintenance and evolution practices, and proper project management principles. The author articulated that individuals could use such development approach to advance their careers. The author compared the standard software engineering method and the agile method that developers usually apply to F/OSSD.

Byron's (2007) research on best practices revealed many reasons that OSS enjoys a slew of advantages over proprietary software. The author noted that when enterprises select open source applications, the organizations could always alter the embedded best practices of the software to suit individual needs. The author opined that because many developers contributed to the software development, higher standards emerge. The author argued that selecting open source software might be the cheapest way to initiate productivity because in some cases the acquisition of the software is "free." Byron (2007) posited however, that whenever developers seek to maximize F/OSSD benefits, they must be willing to change their development approach in fundamental ways.

Cheri, Schaller, and Wilson (n.d.) emphasized how free (not gratuity) and open source software can benefit organizations. The authors attempt to dispel many myths that surround open source software (OSS) development and use regarding software licenses and intellectual property rights. The authors enumerated three perpetual overstated arguments surrounding OSS: code redistribution, license contamination, and intellectual property rights. The authors attempt to allay such often-unfounded fears and attempt to encouraged enterprises to adopt OSS.

Shariff (2006) conducted a presentation that analyzes various considerations that organizations may assess when adapting open source technology. The author enumerated 21 golden rules or best practices that enterprises may use to guide the proper adaption and implementation of OSS within their organization. The author opined that enterprises should start with the big picture, assess expectations, and prepare themselves to manage such expectations. The author noted that centralized control is essential for well-developed systems. Shariff (2006) argued that a crucial step toward secure development is to define workflow and security at the beginning of the project. Shariff (2006) stated that developers should understand the licensing model appropriate for their organization's requirement because such understanding is necessary for selecting the appropriate open source tool to suite the company's needs.

Brydon and Vining (2008) research focused on the role that OSS plays in disrupting established software markets. The authors argued that open source software has long evolved beyond satisfying only small and medium companies. The authors challenged conventional wisdom with two models, one adapted from Fichman and Kemerer (1993) and the other being their enhanced version of the Fichman and Kemerer model. The models depict two distinct stages: incubation and snowball. The authors then expound on how both stages influence the new thrust to open source software selection.

Horwitt (2010) focused on the benefits of database analytics to business intelligence (BI,) that is, how data administrators construct data for analysis as distinct from transaction or other types of management processes. The author noted that because in-data analyses have risen in importance, Gartner included advanced analytics as one of their top 10 strategic technologies for 2010. The author opined that because BI initiatives are playing a more important role in business decisions, the cost of development of such software has reduced drastically over the years allowing small firms to take advantage of the technology. The author stated that if database functions are transparent enough then BI developers could execute complex manipulations of databases. MySQL certainly has a place in this new era for complex queries.

Krill (2009) articulated the sophistication of CouchDB. The author noted that CouchDB store their applications in databases thereby eliminating the need for client-based applications except for a web browser. The author opined that a major benefit of using CouchDB is the ability to synchronize the off-line instances of the software use. MySQL and other open source database installations may reduce the implementation cost of CouchDB.

Hart (2003) noted that schools might benefit from open source technology because they have limited finance, time, and support. Hart (2003) argued that open source technology would seem apt for tackling such issues. The author argued from a historical perspective then outlined how F/OSS can aid educational development. The author emphasized that the culture that surrounds open source is to provide tools that accomplish the job. With the correct tools, the author argued, developers can take development in endless directions. The author also gave a clear distinction between "free" and open source software.

Riehle, Ellenberger, Menahem, Mikhailovski, Natchetoi, Naveh, and Odenwald noted the important role open source software play in the software development industry. The authors opined that enterprises should grasp the development methods used with OSS to build major applications such as SAP or enterprise wide applications. The authors noted that there is no need for competing with the established development methods for proprietary software and the agile method of OSS. The authors further argued that both sets of methods may complement each other. The authors posited that software forges is the best way to engender collaboration, a process common to OSSD.

Weinberg (2006) proffered that the lag of the health care industry behind other industries application and use of information technology no longer has to continue because of the recent convergence of many disparate sectors within the health care industry. The authors noted that with the convergence taking place within the health care industry, enterprise IT vendors have an incentive to foster interoperability and to boost technology within the industry. The authors noted that the cost of such technology innovation and implementation is forcing industries such as health care to consider open source solutions notwithstanding the plethora of standards within the industry.

Lakhani (2006) argued that OSS might be the new model for innovation. The professor argued that open source encourages large-scale scientific problem-solving skill-sets and approaches. The professor opined that because of the transparent nature of open source software development, it provides preamble access and is suitable for collaborative work.

Spinellis (2006) emphasized the use of open source to advance individuals professional career. Spinellis (2006) argued that one of the best ways for developers to grow is to work on existing projects by mending or patching known errors. The author stated that when one joins an existing collaborative community, one is going beyond shaping his or her programming skills; one is shaping his or her communication skills. The author noted that when an individual belongs to an open source collaborative community of practice, such individual exposes himself or herself to respected professionals in the field, therefore networking within the profession might improve the individual's chance of upward mobility within the industry.

Von Krogh and Von Hippel (2006) stated that open source software promise many innovations for both students and practitioners alike. The authors reviewed many of the existing research and assessed the utility of the findings. The authors examined open source research from three perspectives: motivation for contributors; governance, organization, and innovation within various projects; and the competitive dynamics surrounding F/OSSD. The authors also attempted to align the various studies with how open source contributed to the respective disciplines within the management sciences.

Conclusion

Free and open source software (F/OSS) provides many opportunities for enterprises and individuals alike. Carillo and Okolio (2008) noted the importance of F/OSSD within communities of practice and explained how such communities may engage skill-sets to produce usable software. Von Krogh assesses the innovative processes and investors incentives available through F/OSS. Feinberg (2007) articulated IBM and MySQL collaboration and the incentives such collaboration provides to the wider application of F/OSS database use. Mears (2005) opined that moving to open source is borne out of necessity as enterprises grapple with increasing development and maintenance costs of operation.

In a time when economies are underperforming and costs are skyrocketing, enterprises may need to reassess how every investment dollar is spent. Therefore, enterprises will seek new modus operandi. Nomani, et al., (2009) noted that F/OSS provides organizations with flexibility, scalability, and manageability. Brandon (2008) opined that F/OSS has long advanced beyond small or medium firms. Barnett (2004) argued that F/OSS is behind much of the innovation occurring within the software industry. Hammond (2009) noted the renewed interests in F/OSSD as enterprises struggle to manage costs.

F/OSS provides opportunities in many respects. Scacchi (2003) noted that companies of all size participate in F/OSSD. Scacchi (2003) argued that individuals could use F/OSSD to build their careers. Hart (2003) articulated many opportunities available in education when educators incorporate F/OSS in educational development. Riehle, et al., (2009) noted the collaborative benefit of software forges within the F/OSS domain. Weinberg (2006) mentioned the tremendous opportunities available to enterprise IT vendors. Weinberg (2006) noted that IT vendors have an opportunity to foster interoperability and to boost technology within the health care sector. Von Krogh and Von Hippel (2006) noted that F/OSS provides a vast innovative opportunity for students and practitioners alike.

Although there exists some contradictory opinions, the overwhelming view of F/OSSD as an enabler for strategic alignment through tactical and operational factors seem convincing. Through the various summations above, it becomes clear that the open source community provides liberty, equality, fraternity, and camaraderie unheard of in the established propriety software market. The open source community builds stability into their products because developers build what interest them and not just another boring piece of software that nobody really wants. F/OSS is on a journey to be the product of choice when considering strategic alignment for business operations and enabling IT integration whether as factory for existing systems or as a turnaround for enterprise systems development portfolio.

References

Baltzan, P., & Phillips, A. (2009). *Essentials of business driven information systems*. New York, NY: McGraw-Hill Irwin.

Barnett, L. (2004). *Applying open source processes in corporate development organizations*. Retrieved July 16, 2010, from http://enterprise-development.open.collab.net/files/documents/86/28/Forrester_Applying_Open_Source_Processes.pdf

Brydon, M., & Vining, A. R. (2008). Adoption, improvement, and distruption: Predicting the impact of open source applications in enterprise software markets. *Journal of Database Management, 19*(2), 73-94. Retrieved from ProQuest database.

Byron, A. (2007). *Best practices in open source development*. Retrieved July 15, 2010, from

http://www.lullabot.com/articles/best-practices-in-

open-source-development

Carillo, K., & Okoli, C. (2008). The open source

movement: A revolution in software development.

The Journal of Computer Information Systems,

49(2), 1-9. Retrieved from ProQuest database.

Cheri, Y., Schaller, A., & Wilson, G. (n.d.). *Open source*

best practice. Retrieved July 17, 2010, from

http://www.linuxfordevices.com/c/a/Linux-For-

Devices-Articles/Whitepaper-Open-Source-Best-

Practice/

Feinberg, D. (2007). *MySQL will open IBM system i to new*

applications and customers. Retrieved July 15,

2010, from

http://gartner11.gartnerweb.com/resources/148500/

148562/mysql_will_open_ibm_system_i_148562.p

df

Gutierrez, A., Orozco, J., Serrano, A., & Serrano, A. (2006). *Using tactical and operational factors to assess strategic alignment: An SME study.* Retrieved July 8, 2010, from http://citeseerx.ist.psu.edu/

Hammond, J. S. (2009). *Best practices: Improve development effectiveness through strategic adoption of open source.* Retrieved July 15, 2010, from http://www.forrester.com/rb/Research/best_practices_improve_development_effectiveness_through_strategic/q/id/46361/t/2

Hart, T. D. (2003). *Open source in education.* Retrieved July 16, 2010, from http://portfolio.umaine.edu/~hartt/OS%20in%20Education.pdf

Horwitt, E. (2010). *Is in-database analytics an emerging business intelligence (BI) trend?.* Retrieved July 16,

2010, from

http://searchbusinessanalytics.techtarget.com/news/

1506999/Is-in-database-analytics-an-emerging-

business-intelligence-BI-trend

Hoving, R. (2007). Information technology leadership

challenges - past, present, and future. *Information*

Systems Management, 24(2), 147-153. Retrieved

from ProQuest databases

Krill, P. (2009). *CouchDB emerging as a top choice for*

offline web apps. Retrieved July 16, 2010, from

http://www.infoworld.com/d/data-

management/couchdb-emerging-top-choice-offline-

web-apps-777

McLeod, R., & Schell, G. (2007). *Management information*

systems (10 ed.). Upper Saddle River, NJ: Pearson

Prentice Hall.

Mears, J. (2005). *Open source databases grow.* Retrieved

July 14, 2010, from

http://www.networkworld.com/news/2005/082905o

pendb.html?page=1

Nomani, A., Cilimdzic, M., Fadden, S., & Chan, Y. (2009).

Best practices DB2 databases and the IBM general

parallel file system. Retrieved July 16, 2010, from

http://download.boulder.ibm.com/ibmdl/pub/softwa

re/dw/data/bestpractices/DB2BP_GPFS_1009I.pdf

OpenOffice.org. (n.d.). *Why OpenOffice.org.* Retrieved

June 30, 2010, from http://why.openoffice.org/

O'Mahony, S. (2007, June 14). The governance of open

source initiatives: What does it mean to be

community managed?. *Journal of Management and*

Governance, 11(2), 139-150. Retrieved from

EBSCOhost database.

Pavlou, P. A., Housel, T. J., Rodgers, W., & Jansen, E.

(2005, July). Measuring the return on information

technology: A knowledge-based approach for

revenue allocation at the process and firm level.

Journal of the Association for Information Systems,
6(7), 199-226. Retrieved from EBSCOhost
database.

Raymond, E. S. (2000). *The cathedral and the bazaar.*
Retrieved June 30, 2010, from
http://www.catb.org/~esr/writings/cathedral-
bazaar/cathedral-bazaar/

Reese, G. (2002). *Ten mySQL best practices.* Retrieved
July 15, 2010, from http://onlamp.com/lpt/a/2513

Riehle, D., Ellenberger, J., Menahem, T., Mikhailovski, B.,
Natchetoi, Y., Naveh, B., & Odenwald, T. (2009).
Open collaboration within corporations using
software forges. *IEEE Software, 26*(2), 52-58.
Retrieved from ProQuest database.

Scacchi, W. (2003). *Understanding best practices in
free/open source software development.* Retrieved
July 14, 2010, from

http://www.ics.uci.edu/~wscacchi/Presentations/CO

SST/BestPractices.pdf

Shankland, S., Kane, M., & Lemos, R. (2001). *How linux*

saved Amazon millions. Retrieved July 2, 2010,

from http://news.cnet.com/2100-1001-275155.html

Shariff, M. (2006). *Open source best practices*. Retrieved

July 16, 2010, from

http://plone.org/events/conferences/seattle-

2006/presentations/OpenSourceBestPracticses_Mun

war_v1.pdf

Spinellis, D. (2006). Open source and professional

advancement. *IEEE Software, 23*(5), 70-71.

Retrieved from ProQuest database.

Stinebrunner, S. A., Humphrey, T. W., & Davis, J. P.

(2002, October). Benefits, risks, and considerations

in using open licensing. *Licensing Journal*, (9), 15-

23. doi: Retrieved from EBSCOhost database.

Von Krogh, G. (2003, Spring). Open-source software

development. *MIT Sloan Management Review*,

44(3), 14-18. Retrieved from ProQuest database.

Von Krogh, G., & Von Hippel, E. (2006, July). The

promise of research on open source software.

Management Science, 52(7), 975-983. Retrieved

from EBSCOhost database.

Weinberg, B. (2006). *Opinion: Open-source can stretch IT*

health care dollars. Retrieved July 15, 2010, from

http://www.computerworld.com/s/article/9003597/

Opinion_Open_source_can_stretch_IT_health_care

_dollars

Collaboration

Kouzes (2003) argued, "Leadership is an *observable set of skills and abilities*" (Jossey-Bass, 2003, p. xvii) and further stated, "leadership development is self-development" (Jossey-Bass, 2003, p. xviii). Collaboration within such context would therefore help to strengthen systems thinking approach to scholarly analysis, synthesis, and writing because participation in such venture creates self-development. Reed (2006) opined that for one to understand fully, one must go beyond analysis and focus on synthesis. Reed (2006) noted that synthesis involves (1) simple and complex systems that one should properly identify before moving to the next stage (2) assess the entire system, and then (3) contextualize the system properties according to the roles or functions they play within the entire system. Constructivist theory holds that "knowledge are socially produced by communities of people" (Moisseeva, Steinbeck, & Seufert, n.d., p. 1). To this end therefore, collaborative endeavors are immensely beneficial.

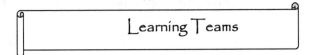

Learning Teams

Information technology (IT) had, is having and will continue to have challenges for the foreseeable future. IT implementation therefore presents many analytical anomalies that IT leaders will only be too eager to obtain clarification and input from others. Hoving (2007) proffered that IT professionals need to ascertain that they are securing the correct technology to address the appropriate business rules and further stated that although IT professionals know the value of IT investments, painfully, the success ratio is not always favorable. Hoving (2007) opined that "IT and business leaders should make both quantifiable business cases and *post-implementation benefit confirmation* [italics added] a routine governance practice (Hoving, 2007, p. 150). The learning team's (LT) "shared competence" (Wenger, 2006, p. 1) will contribute substantially to the quality of an individual's work. The LT is a community that engender relationship and learning as members share knowledge and provide insight into each others perspectives (Wenger, 2006)

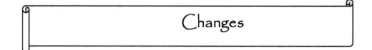

Changes

Feedback contributes to correcting grammar, flawed idea construction, and resource use. One should glean interesting details from suggested references and this may clarify sentences in which the ideas presented were not as clear as they could be. All these rewards are possible when one belongs to a community of practitioners whose experience and exposure to various resources makes it possible to provide constructive feedback and knowledge (Wenger, 2006). In addition, because of the relationship-building taking place within the community of practice, each member can establish personal credibility. "Credibility is the foundation of leadership" (Jossey-Bass, 2003, p. xviii). One can therefore exercise trust in accepting and reacting to the respective suggestions received from the LT because one has faith in such feedback.

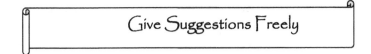

Give Suggestions Freely

Give similar feedback as you received to each team member and provided sources for additional research information. When team members commend you for your input and feedback to their endeavors, and assured you that they will consider such suggestions where appropriate, be genuine in your response. When you genuinely accept and participate in the LT as a community of practice, all members have the opportunity to "bounce ideas off of each other, complete tasks, and work together effectively" ("Transcript of collaborative learning spaces at Missouri University of Science and Technology", n.d., p. 1).

Improving Collaboration

Although one may benefit substantially from collaborating with the LT, I believe that with concerted effort one can better appreciate the four interconnected aspects of collaborative learning and participation within a community of practice. Focus on "Learning as belonging" (Jolliffe, n.d., p. 9) that is, building the necessary relationships and trusts that engender the community spirit. Focus on "learning as becoming" (Jolliffe, n.d., p. 9), that is, appreciating the community for shared value and experience. Focus on "learning as doing" (Jolliffe, n.d., p. 9) through research; and "learning as experience" (Jolliffe, n.d., p. 9) by challenging existing ideas and practices, and advancing new ones.

Conclusion

Collaborating with the LT contributes substantially to the quality of one's research and the content of one's report. One will glean different research ideas from individual members and harness the strengths of each member to prepare a more comprehensive project. Each member should participate in a timely and frank manner with respect and decorum.

Through the experience gained from the LT community of practice, one's general outlook to teamwork should be stronger, and one should become substantially more willing to participate in such ventures in the future.

"The wealth of research into the benefits of learning together cooperatively has been well documented" (Jolliffe, n.d., p. 1). I therefore suggest that collaborative learning and participation within learning teams are mutually beneficial and exceedingly rewarding.

References

Hoving, R. (2007). Information technology leadership

    challenges - past, present, and future. *Information*

    Systems Management, 24(2), 147-153. Retrieved

    from ProQuest databases

Jolliffe, W. (n.d.). *Implementing cooperative learning:*

    developing a network of support. Retrieved July 14,

    2010, from

    http://www.iaie.org/download/turin_paper_jollife.p

    df

Jossey-Bass. (2003). *Business leadership.* San Francisco,

    CA: Author.

Moisseeva, M., Steinbeck, R., & Seufert, S. (n.d.). *Online*

    learning communities and collaborative learning.

    Retrieved July 7, 2010, from

    http://www.iienetwork.org/?p=41543

Reed, G. E. (2006, May/June). Leadership and systems

   thinking. *Defence AT&L, 35*(3), 10-13. Retrieved

   from EBSCOhost databases

Transcript of collaborative learning spaces at Missouri

   University of Science and Technology. (n.d.).

   Retrieved July 14, 2010, from

   http://www.educause.edu/EDUCAUSE+Quarterly/

   EDUCAUSEQuarterlyMagazineVolum/Collaborati

   veLearningSpacesatM/163857

Wenger, E. (2006). *Communities of practice: a brief*

   introduction. Retrieved July 16,2010, from

   http://www.ewenger.com/theory/

4 Questions and Answers

Why Invest in New Technology?

Information systems managers, as do other managers, operate in a context of organizational culture and objectives. Managers play active roles in organizations predetermined by their management positions. "Management is a process that is used to accomplish organizational goals: that is, a process that is used to achieve what an organization wants to achieve" (Luft, 2001, p. 553). For information systems managers to adapt emerging technology therefore, managers must be so empowered. This contemporary approach to empower managers demands a change in organizational abilities, competencies, and directives. Management deals with the complexities of day-to-day operations of a business whereas leaders are change agents (Clawson, 2006).

Empowered information systems leaders do not have to reinvent the wheel. Enough examples exist, both success and failures that decision makers can use to complement their decision-making process. How leaders treat investment in new technology depends on whether managers are capable of deploying disruptive technology or whether they are satisfied with sustaining technology. On the one hand, Polaroid, at its introduction during the 1930s of its instant camera, is seen as a disruptive technology for that given epoch. The instant camera technology was radical, new, and different. The motor vehicle industry, on the other hand, constantly introduces incremental benefits in the form of new models of their motor vehicles whereby not much has changed; maybe an increase in speed, or a smoother ride for passengers (Baltzan & Phillips, 2009).

Advantages/Disadvantages of Pioneering Technology

The Internet and the World Wide Web has created tremendous opportunities for both disruptive and sustaining technologies. Amazon.com has changed the face of how books are bought and sold. It is virtually impossible for a traditional bookstore to stock the number of titles that an online bookstore without any inventory can carry. Ebay is another success story. Ebay has changed the very essence of how an auction is done (Baltzan & Phillips, 2009). Had the leaders of these two ventures taken a sustaining approach they would have missed the overwhelming success that each venture returned.

References

Baltzan, P., & Phillips, A. (2009). *Essentials of business driven information systems*. New York, NY: McGraw-Hill Irwin.

Clawson, J. G. (2006). *Level three leadership: Getting below the surface* (3rd ed.). Upper Sadele River, NJ: Pearson Prentice Hall.

Luft, R. L. (2001, January 1). Management. *Encyclopedia of Business and Finance*, 2, 553-557. Retrieved from EBSCOhost database.

What are the Conditions for Open Source Viability?

The choice of open-source as against proprietary software will remain a contention for some time for both managers and users of information technology resources. This is primarily so because new learning precedes new experiences. According to Raymond (2000), the open-source community (bazaar) enjoys only 5% of skilled programmers whereas the proprietary vendors (cathedral) enjoy the overwhelming 95% (Raymond, 2000). Notwithstanding, bazaar applications presents a unique opportunity to information technology leaders interested in seeing the technology as going beyond departmental support. Such leaders engaged in systems thinking will see the need to traverse beyond analysis and to focus on synthesis of organizational goals and objectives (Reed, 2006).

Information technology implementation traditionally has a high cost factor that is not easily justified through conventional accounting principles. Its justification therefore involves aligning its perceived benefits with improved firm-wide performance (Pavlou, Housel, Rodgers, & Jansen, 2005). Given the foregoing, technology specialists should evaluate anything that may have a direct bearing on information technology implementation for its appropriateness. Open-source applications and operating systems are "free" to acquire. Open-source software is of a high quality given the bazaar implementation methods that such software has endured. Raymond (2000) noted, "... the average quality of software originated in the Linux community is so high" (Raymond, 2000, p. 2).

Cathedral manufacturers such as Microsoft currently control the desktop market with 89.6% of market share (Keizer, 2008). This dominance has been around as of the early 1980s with the introduction of the IBM PCs. One may be familiar with the expression "familiarity breeds contempt." Raymond (2000) said it even better when he quoted Linus Torvalds who quipped, "I'm basically a very lazy person ..." (Raymond, 2000, p. 3).

References

Keizer, G. (2008, December 2). Windows market share

    drops below 90% for first time. *CIO*. Retrieved

    from

    http://www.cio.com/article/467339/Windows_Mark

    et_Share_Drops_Below_90_for_First_Time

Pavlou, P. A., Housel, T. J., Rodgers, W., & Jansen, E.

    (2005, July). Measuring the return on information

    technology: A knowledge-based approach for

    revenue allocation at the process and firm level.

    Journal of the Association for Information Systems,

    6(7), 199-226. Retrieved from EBSCOhost

    database.

Raymond, E. S. (2000). *The cathedral and the bazaar*.

    Retrieved June 30, 2010, from

    http://www.catb.org/~esr/writings/cathedral-

    bazaar/cathedral-bazaar/

Reed, G. E. (2006, May/June). Leadership and Systems

Thinking. *Defense AT&L, 35*(3), 10-13. Retrieved

from EBSCOhost database.

 What Constitute the Free Economy?

The "free economy" especially those affecting or is available to information technology presents many opportunities to individuals and organizations alike. Robust applications covering many business operations are currently available under the GNU Lesser General Public License (LGPL) (OpenOffice.org, n.d.). "OpenOffice.org 3 is the leading open-source office software suite for word processing, spreadsheets, presentations, graphics, databases and more" (OpenOffice.org, n.d., p. 1). OpenOffice.org caters to governments, education, businesses, not for profits, IT businesses, and F/OSS advocates (OpenOffice.org, n.d.). Such "free" productivity software capable of carrying out daily business rules is worthy of serious consideration by information technology specialists. Firms and organizations alike can install OpenOffice.org 3 on many platforms including the Windows operating system (OpenOffice.org, n.d.).

Because open-source applications and operating systems usually involve distribution under the GNU license agreement, there is no issue arising from trademarks, patent, or other intellectual property concerns that can be costly to business operations should any license breach occur. Such intellectual property arrangements present huge opportunities for the information and communication technology sector especially in containing initial capital outlay. An individual, for example, can purchase a $400 personal computer without either an office suite or an operating system from Microsoft. Windows 7 Ultimate operating system currently retails for about $220 and Office Professional 2010 office suite retails for about $500 (Microsoft.com, n.d.). The instant saving of $720 with the installation of the Linux operating system and OpenOffice.org 3 should provide some incentive to such an individual to select the open-source option even to the chagrin of acquiring new knowledge to operate the software. The cost of learning the new operating system and the new application program would likely be less than $720.

For all that is "free" however, there will always be a choice for the expensive (Anderson, n.d.). Notwithstanding, "the trend lines that determine the cost of doing business online all point the same way: to zero" (Anderson, n.d., p. 1).

References

Anderson, C. (n.d.). *Free*. Retrieved June 30, 2010, from

    http://www.wired.com/techbiz/it/magazine/16-

    03/ff_free

Microsoft.com. (n.d.). *Try the new office 2010*. Retrieved

    June 30, 2010, from

    http://www.microsoft.com/en/us/default.aspx

OpenOffice.org. (n.d.). *Licenses*. Retrieved June 30, 2010,

    from http://www.openoffice.org/license.html

OpenOffice.org. (n.d.). *Why OpenOffice.org*. Retrieved

    June 30, 2010, from http://why.openoffice.org/

 How does Collaborative Learning and Content Management Benefit IT?

On the one hand, collaborative learning engages team members to share knowledge and opinions, to respect others viewpoints, to listen attentively, and to maintain membership within the collaborative community. Cooperative learning is therefore a process of building knowledge within a socially acceptable community of members (Moisseeva, Steinbeck, & Seufert, n.d.). On the other hand, content management "combines hardware, software, and infrastructure to enable an organization to store, manage, and access information generated throughout the organization, without regard to its form or source" (Bridges, 2007, p. 30).

One example of how an organization such as an online university is fusing collaboration and content management to achieve given objectives is through the learning teams they create. The objective of the learning teams is to collaborate and brainstorm so that individual members may benefit for his or her personal growth in pursuit of his or her scholarly mission. Learning team members manage to collaborate effectively through conference calls and through web portals.   Group members rely upon the content of the respective postings of each member to prepare his respective assignments. The collaborative approach helps each learner to enrich the quality of work presented to the instructor.

References

Bridges, J. D. (2007, November/December). Taking ECM

from concept to reality. *Information Management

Journal, 41*(6), 30-32,34,36,39. Retrieved from

ProQuest database.

Moisseeva, M., Steinbeck, R., & Seufert, S. (n.d.). *Online

learning communities and collaborative learning.*

Retrieved July 7, 2010, from

http://www.iienetwork.org/?p=41543

What is Innovation of Information Systems?

Innovation in information systems (IS) is the result of adapting new technology, both hardware and software, to an organization to change effectively the modus of its existing business rules (Pearson, Pearson, & Griffin, 2008). The adaptation of such technology may result in either radical or incremental change depending on whether the objective on introducing the new technology is for sustaining or disruptive means. Where the organization implements IS in a way that does not satisfy the existing needs of its customers, such implementation is said to be disruptive. In such circumstance, older markets tend to fail as the emerging markets displace the existing businesses that lack the new technology (Baltzan & Phillips, 2009). Where a business is not as radical in its ideas and decision-making however, information technology managers may choose to improve upon existing technology to the extent that such improvement creates incremental change to business operations and product quality (Baltzan & Phillips, 2009).

Notwithstanding the foregoing, the method to apply when implementing information technology will depend on the strategic decision of the organization. The organization may use both methods at different times during the life of its business. Amazon.com, for example, uses a disruptive technology to change the way book connoisseur and other book buyers purchase their books (Baltzan & Phillips, 2009).

Conclusion

Depending on the strategic mission of an organization, IS may be used to drive business processes or may be applied to create incremental change for business operations. Information systems managers will have to analyze their corporate objectives and implement the best business fit that complement such mission.

References

Baltzan, P., & Phillips, A. (2009). *Essentials of business driven information systems*. New York, NY: McGraw-Hill Irwin.

Pearson, A., Pearson, J. M., & Griffin, C. (2008). Innovating with technology: The impact of overload, autonomy, and work and family conflict. *Journal of Information Technology Theory and Application, 9*(4), 41-65. Retrieved from ProQuest database.

What are Fitness Landscapes?

A landscape typically encompasses three elements. First, there is usually a finite representation set V. Second, the representation set V and the geometrical or topological structure X determines the configuration space, that is, the distance between the various configurations. Third, the fitness/cost function V → R that assigns the various configuration V its actual value (Hordijk, 1998). "These three ingredients together provide a complete mathematical description of fitness landscape, and give rise to the intuitive notion of a more or less rugged landscape" (Hordijk, 1998, p. 4). The theory of fitness landscape originated with evolutionary biologists as they probe the possibility of evolution. The fitness landscape theory arises out of the evolutionary biologists' probity on how the respective species improve fitness over time (Mauboussin & Bartholdson, 2002).

Many existing models capture the essence of the fitness landscape. Three such models include the NK landscapes model that "defines a family of fitness landscapes that can be turned from smooth via rugged to completely random" (Hordijk, 1998, p. 11). Then there is the synchronizing-CA landscape model. This model is the result of the global synchronization of cellular automata. The objective is to establish how one computes arbitrary initial patters from synchronizing the CAs globally (Hordijk, 1998, p. 16). Finally, there is the RNA folding landscapes. "RNA sequences are strings over the alphabet {G,C,A,U} designating the nucleotides guanine, cytosine, adenosine, and uracil (the order in decreasing strength)" (Hordijk, 1998, p. 18).

In applying fitness landscape to businesses, one can think in terms of three landscapes. First, landscapes can be stable in which companies' economic performance is relatively flat. Second, the landscape may be coarse. In a coarse landscape, businesses tolerate change with some amount of predictability. Third, the landscape may be rolling. In a rolling landscape climate, businesses are constantly dealing with change and uncertainty and are invariably evolving through different business approaches (Mauboussin & Bartholdson, 2002). One can also regard these three landscapes as gradual, rugged, and random ("Fitness landscapes", n.d.).

References

Fitness landscapes. (n.d.). Retrieved July 7, 2010, from

http://nextremeformation.com/?p=3056

Hordijk, W. (1998). *Amplitude spectra of fitness*

landscapes. Retrieved July 7, 2010, from

http://citeseerx.ist.psu.edu/viewdoc/summary?doi=1

0.1.1.121.6146

Mauboussin, M. J., & Bartholdson, K. (2002). *Seeking the*

peak: Fitness landscapes and competitive strategy.

Retrieved July 7, 2010, from

http://www.beaconinvest.com/Articles/Seeking%20

the%20Peak.pdf

What is the Importance of Good
Network Design?

Networks are interconnected computers (Curtin, 1997) used to carry out the daily business rules of an organization and to provide information for decision-making and support. Network designs may hamper or enhance businesses in a number of ways. For example, an unstable network may cause downtime resulting in loss of production. Critical applications may bring about savings if they are constantly available for production and use. Network systems may be crucial for time-to-market product and services. Improperly designed and implemented networks may result in high labor cost used for either maintenance or corrective rework (Salazar, 2008).

Because the foregoing plays such crucial role to an organization's failure or success, executives need to understand if the investments in network infrastructure are appropriate for the business. Executives must justify the organization's investment to the respective stakeholders and should therefore account for the "... value, or benefits, of the proposed project" (Salazar, 2008, p. 21) with the assistance of technical experts in the vocation.

Management may examine four primary considerations when assessing network infrastructure. Such issues may include cost of implementation and maintenance, benefits to accrue to the organization through efficiencies and cost savings, flexibility and adaptability of the existing technology to new technology and infrastructure (scalability,) and the risks involved in adapting the technology to prevailing circumstances (Salazar, 2008).

Conclusion

Network infrastructure implementation gives both technocrats and executives an opportunity to liaise with each for a better understanding of information technology use and implementation. Such projects gives management and technicians alike, an opportunity to plan, organize, and motivate each other to achieve the organizations goals and objectives.

References

Curtin, M. (1997). *Introduction to Network Security*.

Retrieved July 14, 2010, from

http://www.interhack.net/pubs/network-security/

Salazar, M. (2008). *The total economic impact of Cisco*

network optimization service. Retrieved July 14,

2010, from

http://www.cisco.com/web/ANZ/netsol/awareness/c

ustomers/assets/pdfs/tei_cisco_nos121008.pdf

What are the Ethics of Wireless
Network Discovery?

Ethics is a branch of philosophy that, at its core, seeks to understand and to determine human actions as right or wrong (Velasquez, Andre, Shanks, & Meyer, 2010). Ethics will therefore vary depending on individuals' interpretation of what they deem correct or incorrect. Open networks are "gray areas in both law and ethics" ("Ethics and legalities of open networks", n.d., p. 1). The best way to assess the arguments advanced for or against accessing someone's open network may be though the use of an analogy. Assuming that my neighbor is playing his radio at a generous volume and I choose to listen along with him, am I stealing, or borrowing bandwidth, or does such circumstance only arise if I broke into his house while he is away and made copies of his CDs ("Ethics and legalities of open networks", n.d.?) Such arguments rely on the values or interpretation of one's ethical principles.

Scanning for wireless network discovery is not illegal according to an FBI advisory (Montcalm, 2003).

"Identifying the presence of a wireless network may not be a criminal violation, however,   there may be criminal violations if the network is actually accessed including theft of   services, interception of   communications,   misuse   of   computing resources, up to and   including violations of the Federal Computer Fraud and Abuse Statute, Theft of Trade   Secrets,   and   other   federal violations" (p. 6).

Notwithstanding, the legality of the act does not necessarily make such an act ethical, but therein lies the real problem. Too many areas of law may possibly conflict with ethics. Assume that I entered an establishment that offers free Internet but I unintentionally connect to an individual's private network that lives across the road, should anyone blame me (Montcalm, 2003, p. 10)?

References

Ethics and legalities of open networks. (n.d.). Retrieved
July 14, 2010, from
http://etutorials.org/Mac+OS/mac+os+x+unwired/C
hapter+4.+Wi-
Fi+on+the+Road/4.2+Ethics+and+Legalities+of+O
pen+Networks/

Montcalm, E. (2003). *How to avoid ethical and legal issues
in wireless network discovery*. Retrieved July 14,
2010, from
http://www.sans.org/reading_room/whitepapers/wir
eless/avoid-ethical-legal-issues-wireless-network-
discovery_176

Velasquez, M., Andre, C., Shanks, T., & Meyer, M. J.
(2010). *What is ethics?*. Retrieved July 14, 2010,
from

http://www.scu.edu/ethics/practicing/decision/whati

sethics.html

 What are 4G Broadband?

Wireless networks consist of many access points (AP) used to support simultaneous users of mobile computing demand (Raghavendra, Belding, Papagiannaki, & Almeroth, 2010). The shrewdness and intelligence of modern mobile users however, continue to drive demand for faster, secure, and less costly wireless services. Because of the liberalized telecommunication sector, competition forces wireless providers to respond to customer demands in a timely manner and at a competitive cost ("Maximizing the wireless network evolution with WiMAX", 2007).

The first generation (*1G*) of wireless broadband operated primarily on the 900 MHz frequency. The technology provides access through the total access communication system (TACS) protocol. The technology also provided access through the advanced mobile phone system (AMPS,) and the extended total access communication systems (ETACS) protocol ("Mobile Telephony", n.d.). Second generation (*2G*) of mobile networks include global system for mobile communications (GSM – 2G, 9.6kbps,) general packet radio service (GPRS – 2.5G, 114Kbits/s,) and enhanced data rates for GSM evolution (EDGE – 2.75G, 384 Kbps) operating on the 900, 1800, and 1900 MHz bands. The *2G* standard also operates on code division multiple access (CDMA) and time division multiple access (TDMA) standards ("Mobile Telephony", n.d.). GSM operates at a range of about 22 miles whereas GPRS and EDGE operates at a range of about 18 miles.

A comparison between the third (*3G*) and fourth (*4G*) generations of mobile computing indicate that both *3G* and *4G* operate between a bandwidth of 5-20 MHz. *3G* provides access on wideband CDMA and *4G* provide access on Multi-carrier CDMA or TDMA ("4G wireless standard", n.d.). Both technologies operate within a range of about 18 and 124 miles respectively.

According to Geppert (n.d.), "It is certainly much less expensive to retain a customer than to go out and acquire a new customer" (Geppert, n.d., p. 1). Telecommunication companies must therefore respond to customer needs swiftly. Geppert (n.d.) noted pricing continue to fall because of the competitive market and customer demands. Geppert (n.d.) noted that consumers continue to demand reduced prices as companies compete and offer low cost services to make their customers happy.

References

4G wireless standard. (n.d.). Retrieved July 20, 2010, from

http://www.nd.edu/~mhaenggi/NET/wireless/4G/

Geppert, C. (n.d.). *Global trends in wireless & broadband.*

Retrieved July 20, 2010, from

http://www.kpmg.com/Global/en/IssuesAndInsights

/ArticlesPublications/Commwatch/Pages/Global-

Trends-Wireless-Broadband.aspx

Maximizing the wireless network evolution with WiMAX.

(2007). Retrieved July 20, 2010, from

http://www.motorola.com/staticfiles/Business/Produ

cts/Wireless%20Broadband%20Networks/WiMAX/

WiMAX%20Access%20Points/WAP%20600/_Doc

uments/Static_files/Maximizing_the_Wireless_Net

work_Evolution_with_WiMAX_White_Paper.pdf?l

ocaleId=52

Mobile Telephony. (n.d.). Retrieved July 20, 2010, from

http://en.kioskea.net/contents/telephonie-

mobile/reseaux-mobiles.php3

Raghavendra, R., Belding, E. M., Papagiannaki, K., &

Almeroth, K. C. (2010). *Unwanted link layer traffic*

in large IEEE 802.11 wireless networks. Retrieved

July 20, 2010, from

http://www.computer.org/portal/web/tmc

Are there Opportunities for Blogging?

Many professionals, organizations, and individuals are using "social computing technologies such as wikis, blogs, and microblogs" (SCT) (Pikas, 2009, p. 1) to convey information and to encourage participation in discussion, and idea generation. On the one hand, wikis are read/write medium to encourage community participation. On the other hand, blogs are discrete posts arranged in reverse chronological order (Pikas, 2009). Within certain context, therefore, a particular type of social computing is more appropriate.

Wikis, for example, encourage editing of content by "anyone" (Pikas, 2009, p. 1) gaining access to such data. Assuming that an organization has a scholarly, practical focus, such organization may wish not to use wikis as their method of provoking thought because in a scholarly context, peer-review plays the ultimate role for scholarly worth within the discipline. Blogs would suite such a circumstance much better than wikis. Organizations wishing to encourage a wide participation however, may find it more pleasing to use wikis as their mode of collaborative endeavor.

All SCT or social networks carry certain rewards including immediacy, expertise location, find-ability/archiving, collaboration, and personal information management (PIM) (Pikas, 2009). Threats may include promotion, tenure, credit, attrition, authority, and intellectual property (Pikas, 2009). Specific benefits accruing to the business community operating blogs may include many characteristics. For example, blogs are quick and easy to set up. They are inexpensive to operate. They provide easy access to company news. They are search engine friendly. They are easily accessible. They may appear authoritative. They encourage brand awareness.

They build upon collaboration within a community of practice. They allow businesses to understand their stakeholders much better, and they reduce the need for traditional communication methods (Jackson, 2006).

References

Jackson, M. (2006). *10 big benefits of a busy business blog (and how to take advantage)*. Retrieved July 21, 2010, from

http://www.webreference.com/authoring/bus_blog/

Pikas, C. (2009). *Test essay 3: Blogs, wikis, microblogging & benefits/threats to science communication*. Retrieved July 21, 2010, from

http://scienceblogs.com/christinaslisrant/2009/05/test_essay_3_blogs_wikis_micro.php

What are the Benefits of SaaS and Cloud Computing?

The du jour phrase cloud computing seem to conjure such diverse and even conflicting meaning among computer professionals. To some, cloud computing represents an "updated version of utility computing: basically virtual servers available over the internet" (Knorr & Gruman, 2008, p. 1). Enterprises use utility computing for "supplemental, non-mission-critical needs" (Knorr & Gruman, 2008, p. 2). To others however, cloud computing encompass anything an enterprise achieve through information technology that falls outside the realm of the company's firewall. Such proponents usually include outsourced projects as part of the definition (Knorr & Gruman, 2008).

SaaS

Software as a service (SaaS) is a special type of cloud computing that use the browser to provide an application to many customers (Knorr & Gruman, 2008), typically providing each tenant with their own database (Chong, Carraro, & Wolter, 2006). SaaS has two main categories: (1) line of business services or "business solutions offered to companies and enterprises, and sold or made available to these enterprises on a subscription basis" ("SaaS", n.d., p. 1) and (2) customer-oriented services offered to the public either freely or through paid subscription ("SaaS, n.d.).

Corporations such as SalesForce.com with their customer relationship management (CRM) software, and Google with Google Apps, are two enterprises that use SaaS to leverage business costs for their customers (Cusumano, 2010).

References

Chong, F., Carraro, G., & Wolter, R. (2006). *Multi-tenant data architecture*. Retrieved July 21, 2010, from http://msdn.microsoft.com/en-us/library/aa479086.aspx

Cusumano, M. (2010, April). Technology strategy and management: Cloud computing ans SaaS as new computing platforms. *Communications of the ACM*, 27-29. doi: 10.1145/1721654.1721667

Knorr, E., & Gruman, G. (2008). *What cloud computing really means*. Retrieved July 21, 2010, from http://www.infoworld.com/print/34031

SaaS. (n.d.). Retrieved July 21, 2010, from http://www.tech-faq.com/saas.html

What is Business Intelligence and Intellectual Property?

Business intelligence (BI) is often seen as an advanced stage of decision support systems (DSS) for enterprise reporting. "BI is a broad category of applications and technologies for gathering, storing, analyzing, and providing access to data to help enterprise users make better business decisions" (Brannon, 2010, p. 2). BI usually involves the use of data warehouse and data marts, various reporting and analytics tools, to assist management and executives to make better and more informed decisions (Brannon, 2010).

A current trend in BI is the use of in-database analytics. Enterprises, both small and large can use advanced analytics tools to assess financial strategies and risk management (Horwitt, 2010). Horwitt (2010) noted, "in-database analytics has significantly bolstered this BI trend by making such applications affordable to organizations that can't afford either supercomputers or on-staff quantitative analysts" (Horwitt, 2010, p. 1).

Intellectual Property

Intellectual property are "creations of the mind: inventions, literary and artistic works, symbols, names and images used in commerce" (Wood, 2006, p. 1). Intellectual property may incorporate patents, trademarks, copyrights, industrial designs, know-how, trade secrets, plant varieties, trade dress, layout designs, integrated circuits, related rights, geographical indications, traditional knowledge, database rights (Europe), domain names, and genetic resources (Wood, 2006, p. 5).

Management need to be especially aware of intellectual property rights to avoid violating such rights and responsibilities. Rights may include the right to distribute, the right to source code, or the right to modify the existing software (Stinebruner, Humphrey, & Davis, 2002). Responsibilities may include an offer of license to others granting the same rights accrue to the license, and notice of the terms of the license (Stinebruner et al., 2002).

References

Brannon, N. (2010, July). Business intelligence and E-discovery. *Intellectual Property & Technology Law Journal, 22*(7), 1-5. Retrieved from EBSCOhost database.

Horwitt, E. (2010). *Is in-database analytics an emerging business intelligence (BI) trend?*. Retrieved July 16, 2010, from http://searchbusinessanalytics.techtarget.com/news/1506999/Is-in-database-analytics-an-emerging-business-intelligence-BI-trend

Stinebruner, S. A., Humphrey, T. W., & Davis, J. P. (2002, October). Benefits, risks, and considerations in using open licensing. *Licensing Journal, 22*(9), 15-24. Retrieved from EBSCOhost databases.

Wood, J. (2006, January). *Defining intellectual property rights (IPRs)*. Paper presented at the University lecture, Kingston, Jamaica.

What is Simulation-based Acquisition?

Simulation-based acquisition entails tools and technologies that allow enterprises to share modeling (simplified temporal representation of a system that will aid understanding) and simulation (manipulation of model to capture temporal representation) to ultimately optimize performance (Criscimagna, n.d.). This is a feat more suitable for large enterprises such as fortune 500 companies and government agencies.

References

http://www.phpmyadmin.net/home_page/index.php

Criscimagna, N. H. (n.d.). *Simulation-based acquisition (SBA)*. Retrieved July 27, 2010, from

http://www.theriac.org/DeskReference/viewDocument.php?id=221

What is Crowd Sourcing and Cognitive Surplus?

The popularity of crowd sourcing is increasing, as enterprises understand better its contribution to profitability (Watson, 2009). Howe (as cited in Watson, 2009) described crowd sourcing as "the act of a company or institution taking a function once performed by employees and outsourcing it to an undefined (and generally large) network of people in the form of an open call" (Watson, 2009, p. 1). This definition implies that a massive amount of persons can do a job previously executed by employees at a low cost. In addition, innovative ideas may come from the plethora of participation engaged in the project (Watson, 2009). Organizations can therefore use crowd sourcing to seek solutions especially in challenging areas in which the answers may not be obvious.

Academia seems to be leading the way with crowd sourcing by building many databases. GroupEye is a project for college students seeking gigs. Indiana University use crowd sourcing to alleviate its IT helpdesk costs. The Los Angeles Unified School District use crowd sourcing to teach K-8 students language arts and math, and Champlain College initiated a Champlain For Reel program in 2009 ("10 awesome examples of crowd sourcing in the college classroom", 2010).

Cognitive Surplus

Cognitive surplus addresses "the surplus brain power available as a result of the free time made possible through technology advances, cultural changes, and new politico-social arrangements" ("Cognitive surplus: "Collective intelligence" or "Organizing wisdom"?", 2009, p. 1). The crowd could undoubtedly use cognitive surplus in ways that create knowledge and skill-sets relevant to specific and the wider market needs. This process is already occurring; teenagers today watch less television than in the past, and spend a vast number of hours contributing to online activities (Chatfield, 2010).

References

10 awesome examples of crowd sourcing in the college

classroom. (2010). Retrieved July 28, 2010, from

http://www.onlineuniversities.com/blog/2010/07/10

-awesome-examples-of-crowdsourcing-in-the-

college-classroom/

Chatfield, T. (2010). *Cognitive surplus by Clay Shirky*.

Retrieved July 28. 2010, from

http://www.guardian.co.uk/books/2010/jun/27/cogn

itive-surplus-clay-shirky-book-review

Cognitive surplus: "Collective intelligence" or "Organizing

wisdom"?. (2009). Retrieved July 28, 2010, from

http://blog.crossoverhealth.com/2009/01/27/cogniti

ve-surplus-collective-intelligence-or-organizing-

wisdom/

Watson, A. (2009). *Advantages and disadvantages of*

crowd sourcing. Retrieved July 28, 2010, from

http://www.prlog.org/10369393-advantages-and-disadvantages-of-crowd-sourcing.pdf

How Does Disruptive Technology Influence Software Development?

When organizations introduce technology and products that existing customers did not realize they need, such organizations are taking a disruptive approach to their business strategy. Organizations so inclined often introduce new products and markets with such technology, effectively eliminating existing businesses and markets over time (Baltzan & Phillips, 2009). Existing markets tend to rely on sustaining technology whereby the enterprises focus on incremental improvements in their product line and use of technology (Baltzan & Phillips, 2009).

Disruptive technology may have devastating effects on existing businesses, for example, revolutionizing the book markets with their online store, Amazon.com choose to disrupt yet again those who have joined the fray.

Amazon.com introduces open source technology in autumn 2001 shaving "millions of dollars from its technology costs" (Shankland, Kane, & Lemos, 2001, p. 1) effectively maintaining its dominant position in the marketplace. Although one may argue that this second phase of disruption is not as overwhelming as the introduction of the online store itself, when put into perspective of the global economic decline and increased competition, Amazon.com has taken clear steps ahead of its competitors to stay "alive" forcing others to either follow suit or diminish over time.

Microsoft, a major software developer and distributor, has seen a reduction in its market share because of the increasing pervasive presence of open source software. Because of the growth of open source operating system, Microsoft, for the first time, have seen its market share reduced below 90% in December 2008

(Keizer, 2008). However, Microsoft has long anticipated such an effect upon their business. Microsoft approached the Securities and Exchange Commission (SEC) as early as 2003 warning them of the devastation that open source may pose on its current business practices. Microsoft conceded that they might have to lower cost to stay in business (Galli, 2002). Technology specialists may count on such blessings as a direct result of the disruption created by free and open source software development (F/OSSD).

References

Baltzan, P., & Phillips, A. (2009). *Essentials of business driven information systems*. New York, NY: McGraw-Hill Irwin.

Galli, P. (2002, February 3). Microsoft warns SEC of open-source threat. *eWeek.com*. Retrieved from http://www.eweek.com/c/a/Application-Development/Microsoft-Warns-SEC-of-OpenSource-Threat/

Keizer, G. (2008). *Windows market share drops below 90% for the first time*. Retrieved June 30, 2010, from http://www.cio.com/article/467339/Windows_Market_Share_Drops_Below_90_for_First_Time

Shankland, S., Kane, M., & Lemos, R. (2001). *How linux saved Amazon millions*. Retrieved July 2, 2010, from http://news.cnet.com/2100-1001-275155.html

What is the Danger with Ambiguity and Systems Development?

Information technology (IT) is constantly evolving creating new capabilities and approaches to solving business problems at an increasing rate (Kautz, Madsen, & Norbjerg, 2007). "The tools, techniques, and processes used for producing information systems (IS) are undergoing profound changes as well" (Kautz et al., 2007, p. 217). Such fact does not negate the methodological approach necessary for completing successful IT projects. The analysis and design teams should properly assess and understand business users, requirements, and design, define workflow configuration and coordination, and adapt appropriate evaluation and maintenance methods (Scacchi, 2003).

Where correct and methodological approaches are followed, design teams will likely detect ambiguity and execute the proper response during the appropriate stages of analysis and design. However, information systems development (ISD) is a great deal more complex than dealing with ambiguity problems. Issues such as skills and organizations matter to the quality and success of a project. The challenges outlined in paragraph one demand new skills from both the development teams and end users (Kautz et al., 2007). Prior to the age of the World Wide Web, for example, the needs for ISD teams were quite different from what they are at present. Web-based designs have special requirements such as "information architect, multimedia designer and multimedia project manager" (Kautz et al., 2007, p. 220).

There must be a concerted effort to clarify ambiguity but because of many contending interests in ISD, the challenge to be successful bears heavily on CIOs and project managers. Management should therefore clearly understand the project scope and the strategic fit

within business organizations, and implement the

appropriate methods for a successful ISD.

References

Kautz, K., Madsen, S., & Norbjerg, J. (2007, July).

Presistent problems and practices in information

systems development. *Information Systems Journal,*

17(3), 217-239. Retrieved from EBSCOhost

database.

Scacchi, W. (2003). *Understanding best practices in*

free/open source software development. Retrieved

July 14, 2010, from

http://www.ics.uci.edu/~wscacchi/Presentations/CO

SST/BestPractices.pdf

NOTES